WWW.APEXEDITIONS.COM

Copyright © 2022 by Apex Editions, Mendota Heights, MN 55120. All rights reserved. No part of this book may be reproduced or utilized in any form or by any means without written permission from the publisher.

Apex is distributed by North Star Editions:
sales@northstareditions.com | 888-417-0195

Produced for Apex by Red Line Editorial.

Photographs ©: Shutterstock Images, cover (bird), 1 (bird), 4–5, 6–7, 8–9, 10–11, 12, 13, 14–15, 16–17, 18, 19, 20–21, 22–23, 24–25, 26, 27, 29; Unsplash, cover (background), 1 (background)

Library of Congress Control Number: 2021915670

ISBN
978-1-63738-147-2 (hardcover)
978-1-63738-183-0 (paperback)
978-1-63738-254-7 (ebook pdf)
978-1-63738-219-6 (hosted ebook)

Printed in the United States of America
Mankato, MN
012022

NOTE TO PARENTS AND EDUCATORS

Apex books are designed to build literacy skills in striving readers. Exciting, high-interest content attracts and holds readers' attention. The text is carefully leveled to allow students to achieve success quickly. Additional features, such as bolded glossary words for difficult terms, help build comprehension.

TABLE OF CONTENTS

CHAPTER 1
HUNTING AT NIGHT 5

CHAPTER 2
LIFE IN THE WILD 11

CHAPTER 3
ALL KINDS OF OWLS 17

CHAPTER 4
CATCHING PREY 23

Comprehension Questions • 28

Glossary • 30

To Learn More • 31

About the Author • 31

Index • 32

CHAPTER 1

HUNTING AT NIGHT

A barn owl sits in a hollow tree. The night is dark and quiet. But the owl hears a rustling sound. Its sharp eyes spot a mouse scurrying along the ground below.

A barn owl's face is shaped like a heart. This shape helps send sound to the owl's ears.

The owl's long wings fan out. It swoops silently down toward the grass.

Owls don't flap their wings as often as other large birds do.

Owls have wide wings with soft feathers. This lets them flap slowly and quietly.

An owl's light body and large wings help it carry prey.

The owl grabs the mouse with its **talons**. Then it returns to its tree and swallows the mouse whole.

OWL SOUNDS

Many owls hoot. Some owls whistle, hiss, chirp, or sing. The sounds have different meanings. They may signal danger. Young owls also call for food.

CHAPTER 2

LIFE IN THE WILD

Owls are found all over the world. They often live in deserts, grasslands, or forests. Some owls **migrate** to search for food.

Snowy owls live in cold, northern areas.

11

Some owls make their homes in hollow trees.

Most owls find **mates** in late fall or early spring. Together, they find a nest or hollow.

Male owls show off for females. They fluff their feathers, dance, or offer food.

Burrowing owls make or find holes in the ground.

Female owls lay eggs. When the eggs hatch, the owlets are small and helpless. Their parents feed and care for them. After a month or two, owlets can fly and live on their own.

DIFFERENT AGES

Owls lay eggs a few days apart, so the owlets hatch at different times. The oldest owlets are the strongest. They usually grab the most food.

Baby owls have soft, fluffy feathers. Later, they grow new feathers that allow them to fly.

CHAPTER 3

ALL KINDS OF OWLS

There are about 250 **species** of owls. All have flat, round faces. Many have **tufts** on their ears.

The great horned owl is named for the long tufts of feathers on the sides of its head.

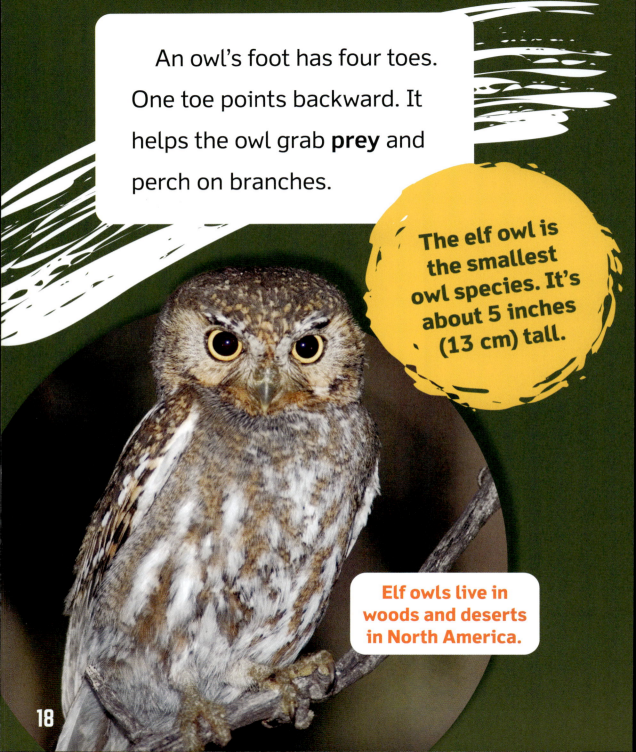

An owl's foot has four toes. One toe points backward. It helps the owl grab **prey** and perch on branches.

The elf owl is the smallest owl species. It's about 5 inches (13 cm) tall.

Elf owls live in woods and deserts in North America.

Blakiston's fish owls grab fish from rivers and lakes.

The Blakiston's fish owl grows nearly 28 inches (71 cm) tall. It's the largest owl species.

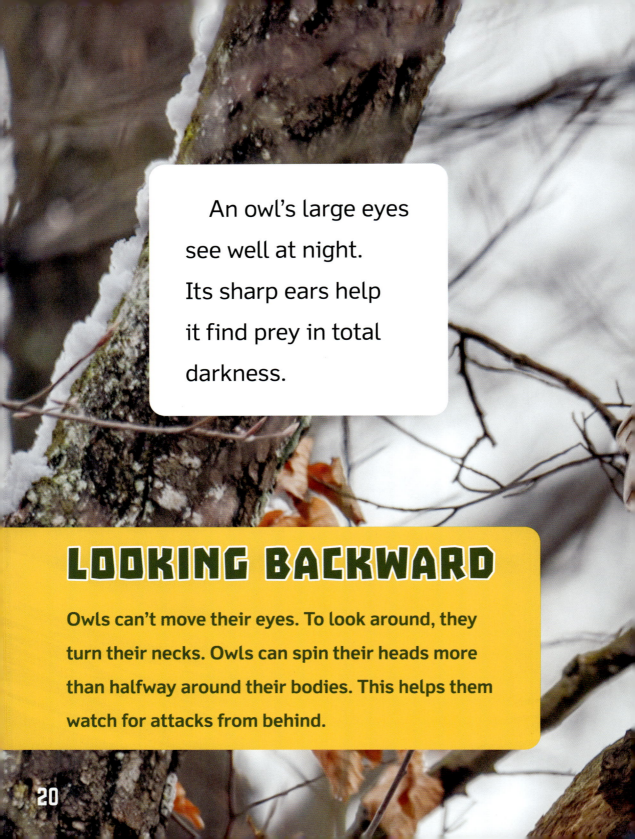

An owl's large eyes see well at night. Its sharp ears help it find prey in total darkness.

LOOKING BACKWARD

Owls can't move their eyes. To look around, they turn their necks. Owls can spin their heads more than halfway around their bodies. This helps them watch for attacks from behind.

Ural owls sit and watch for prey in forests.

CATCHING PREY

Most owls eat **rodents** and other small animals. Owls may eat fish and **reptiles**, too. Some even eat other birds.

Many owls eat rats and mice. Great horned owls can catch larger animals, such as rabbits.

Most owls hunt at night. Some owls spot prey from trees. They swoop down to grab it. Other owls hunt while flying. Some even chase prey on the ground.

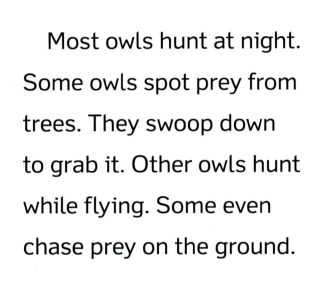

DAYTIME OWLS

A few owls hunt by daylight. One is the northern pygmy-owl. This owl sits and waits for prey. Other daytime hunters include the northern hawk owl and snowy owl.

The northern pygmy-owl hides in trees to catch songbirds.

Owls kill prey with their talons and beaks. They eat the whole animal, even the bones. After meals, owls spit up the parts they cannot **digest**.

Owls often gulp down small animals in one bite.

The bunch of fur and bones that owls spit up is called a pellet.

Sometimes, owls hide food after they catch it. They come back later to eat.

COMPREHENSION QUESTIONS

Write your answers on a separate piece of paper.

1. Write a sentence describing one way owls hunt their prey.

2. Owls can live in both hot and cold places. Which type of place would you prefer to live in? Why?

3. Which body part do only some owls have?

    A. wide, flat faces

    B. large tufts on their ears

    C. four toes on each foot

4. How would flying quietly help an owl catch prey?

    A. The owl can sneak up on prey and surprise it.

    B. The owl can hoot to scare its prey instead.

    C. The owl can't fly as fast as its prey.

5. What does **swoops** mean in this book?

*The owl's long wings fan out. It **swoops** silently down toward the grass.*

    A. makes loud noises
    B. flies high into the air
    C. flies smoothly down

6. What does **signal** mean in this book?

*The sounds have different meanings. They may **signal** danger.*

    A. to cause something to happen
    B. to say everything is safe
    C. to give a message or warning

Answer key on page 32.

GLOSSARY

digest
To break down food so the body can get energy from it.

mates
Pairs of animals that come together to have babies.

migrate
To move from one part of the world to another.

prey
An animal that is hunted and eaten by another animal.

reptiles
Cold-blooded animals that have scales.

rodents
Small, furry animals with large front teeth, such as rats or mice.

species
A group of animals or plants that are similar and can breed with one another.

talons
Long, sharp claws that birds use to hunt.

tufts
Bunches of fur or feathers that stick up.

TO LEARN MORE

BOOKS

Sommer, Nathan. *Owls*. Minneapolis: Bellwether Media, 2019.

Whipple, Annette. *Whooo Knew? The Truth About Owls.* New York: Reycraft Books, 2020.

Wilson, Mark. *Owling: Enter the World of the Mysterious Birds of the Night.* North Adams, MA: Storey Publishing, 2019.

ONLINE RESOURCES

Visit **www.apexeditions.com** to find links and resources related to this title.

ABOUT THE AUTHOR

Golriz Golkar is a former elementary school teacher. She has written more than 40 nonfiction books for children. She loves to sing and spend time with her daughter.

INDEX

B
barn owl, 5
beaks, 26
Blakiston's fish
   owl, 19

E
ears, 17, 20
eggs, 14
elf owl, 18
eyes, 5, 20

F
feathers, 7, 13
food, 9, 11, 13–14,
   27

H
heads, 20
hunting, 24

N
nests, 12
northern hawk
   owl, 24
northern
   pygmy-owl, 24

P
prey, 18, 20, 24, 26

S
snowy owl, 24
species, 17–19

T
talons, 9, 26
toes, 18
trees, 5, 9, 24

W
wings, 6–7

Answer Key:
1. Answers will vary; **2.** Answers will vary; **3.** B; **4.** A; **5.** C; **6.** C